# EXTRAVAGANT GRACE
## HOW I GAVE BIRTH FOUR TIMES WITHOUT PAIN

### SANDY BILONG

GREAT BOOKS

First published by GREAT Books 2021

Copyright © 2021 by Sandy Bilong

All rights reserved. No part of this publication may be reproduced, stored or transmitted in any form or by any means, electronic, mechanical, photocopying, recording, scanning, or otherwise without written permission from the publisher. It is illegal to copy this book, post it to a website, or distribute it by any other means without permission.

Sandy Bilong asserts the moral right to be identified as the author of this work.

Scripture quotations from The Authorized (King James) Version. Rights in the Authorized Version in the United Kingdom are vested in the Crown. Reproduced by permission of the Crown's patentee, Cambridge University Press

Scripture quotations are from The ESV® Bible (The Holy Bible, English Standard Version®), copyright © 2001 by Crossway, a publishing ministry of Good News Publishers. Used by permission. All rights reserved.

First edition

Editing by Khalea Queen
Cover art by Ulrish Bitounou
Front/Back Cover Photo by Dylan Palanga

This is an amazing story of God's extravagant grace. A story that will inspire you to trust God more than you ever have. A woman believes that God will bless her to have her children supernaturally, and then gives birth, not once, but four times, painlessly. Once, even while laughing! If God will be so gracious to Sandrine, He stands ready to be gracious to you. Trust Him.

-Bishop Darlingston G. Johnson
**Presiding Prelate Harvest Intercontinental Ministries - Unlimited**

Extravagant Grace is an excellent read. Throughout the book, we see the hand of God move in very powerful ways. I believe anyone who reads this book will truly grow to appreciate how God's love is always available no matter who you are or where you've come from. His grace knows no boundaries is what you will learn as you read through the pages.

-**Pastor Varney Taylor, International Director of Youth and Young Adult Ministries HIM-U**

Extravagant Grace is a must read. I endorse this book because it clearly describes a beautiful journey of an ordinary lady who experiences God's grace in an exuberant fashion. The author helps us understand and appreciate how great our God is and that anyone could believe and experience His grace in different areas of our lives. This is a breathtaking story that I recommend to all. My faith has moved up to a higher level, knowing that this God is not a respecter of persons, and we can and should believe Him for anything. Thank you Sandrine for being so transparent and allowing us to see the extent of God's love for us and how far He will go to appropriate His favor on us.

-**Dr/Minister Patricia B. Ayuk**
**Associate Professor- Howard University College of Pharmacy**

*This book is a great read for young mothers about to start their families. It gives an entertaining account of a woman, Sister Sandrine and other women in labour. Extravagant Grace is a real testimony of God's grace. It reminds us that grace is always present, but it is our personal faith in God that will make it evident. A good spirit filled read, great as a study on grace. Thanks for this wonderful blessing.*
-**Joanne Phillips Spencer**


*Extravagant Grace is written with such truthfulness and grace! This book will cause the unbeliever to Believe in Jesus – Christ and his Grace.*
-**Gwendylon Gray-Pompey Mensah**


*This was such a great read! It was so encouraging to read of the evidence of God's Grace woven throughout Sandrine's story/testimony. Sandrine is a great story teller and it is evident in this book. You will definitely be encouraged after reading this book and become more aware of God's grace being evident in your own life.*
-**Melissa Teage**
**Transition Specialist at Montgomery County Public Schools**

*Your story and testimony is intense and miraculous.*
-**Pastor Zangai Peabody**
**Director of Discipleship & Men Services**

*Thanks to the person of the Holy Spirit, my best friend.
To my sons, Wilfried and Yvan,
and my daughters, Joy and Grace,
who will always remember that
the grace of God wins.*

# Contents

| | | |
|---|---|---|
| *Foreword* | | ii |
| *Acknowledgement* | | v |
| 1 | My Origins | 1 |
| 2 | Labor Pains Are Real | 7 |
| 3 | A Love Story | 14 |
| 4 | My Prayer Partner | 20 |
| 5 | A Cult or a Husband? | 24 |
| 6 | My Story of No Labor Pains: The Birth of Willy | 27 |
| 7 | The Birth of Yvan | 31 |
| 8 | The Birth of Joy | 41 |
| 9 | The Birth of Grace | 46 |
| 10 | Conclusion - Lessons From My Story | 51 |
| 11 | Testimonies | 59 |
| *Salvation* | | 63 |
| *About the Author* | | 64 |

# Foreword

Two important events caused me to write this book. The first is the powerful message I received from my senior pastor on the revelation of the grace of God in my life. The second is the painful 13-hour labor my little sister went through during the birth of my nephew.

The first time I came across the notion of grace was when I was born again and became a child of God. *"You are saved by grace through faith"* is a statement that was quite abstract to me at the beginning of my faith, but I trusted the men of God and just believed without understanding what it really meant. At some point in my faith journey, I heard men of God preach about grace, but since I had not seen it practically, I was still not grasping the concept. However, I knew that God could do what He wanted and even do above all that we can think or imagine.

Religiously, I would say, *"By the Grace of God,"* I was able to do this or that. I remember using that expression all the time just as a habit to sound spiritual. It was only when I moved to Maryland that I began grasping the message of grace in the church. Then, my senior pastor, Bishop Darlingston G. Johnson, broke down grace in a comprehensible way that all the members could grasp and embrace. Recently, he wrote a book titled *Grace That Overcomes*, and that book and his teachings led me to a greater revelation of grace. One day, he taught on extravagant grace, and that message touched my heart in such a way that God started revealing to me what that grace was about.

Here are some quotes from his book: *"Grace is God blessing us not because we are good, but because He is good... Grace is God giving you a new life, God operating a DNA transplant... Grace is God showing me His reckless love no matter how much I sin... Grace is God Making dead men Live again."*

What did I understand from these quotes?

*"Grace is God blessing us not because we are good, but because He is good."*

When I read this quote, it humbled me. I saw the book of my life open in front of me and God showed me all the things I had done in my life that were not glorifying Him. He showed me all the hatred, jealousy, wickedness that had been my lifestyle through many years but still, he showed me mercy. He blessed me with uncountable blessings not because of me, but because of Himself.

*"Grace is God giving us a new DNA, making dead men live again."*

After reading this quote, I realized that I had no life before I gave my life to Christ. I was without hope and condemned to hell, but God saved me from eternal death. I also realized how much the Word of God transformed me.

In addition to the message of my senior pastor, another trigger was the birth of my nephew. On the 4th day of August, my little sister called me from Cameroon and told me that she was going into labor. It was about 8 pm when she called me and said, *"those contractions are not a joke."* After 30 minutes, her husband told me she was in so much pain that she could not even answer the phone. I felt powerless at that point. I was asking myself questions as to why—why was she in labor for thirteen good hours only to finally have a C-section?

Then the Lord started to minister to me. I could hear His voice in my heart telling me how blessed I had been, and how His grace had surrounded me all these years even before I was born again. He then took me back to the time when I was born and reminded me of how He protected me and kept me.

If you are a child of God, as you read this book, I believe in Jesus that you will get to experience the extravagant grace of God the same way I did. For His glory, God will use you mightily in ways that you cannot imagine.

If you don't have a relationship with Jesus Christ or have not given your life to Him, I pray that my story will help you to discover the extravagant grace of God. Through my story, I pray that you get to understand who Jesus is and accept Him as the ONLY way, that you surrender your entire life to Him as your Lord and Savior, and that you choose to live for Him, in order to fulfill the purpose for which He created you.

# Acknowledgement

My special thanks to my darling husband, Casimir, for his constant love and support, for reading, editing, and providing unwavering support towards this project.

My thanks to Pastor Chrys Johnson, our Senior Pastor, for reading this manuscript, reviewing, encouraging, and providing advice.

Thanks to my Senior Pastor Bishop Darlingston G. Johnson for the message of Grace that changed my life forever.

Thanks to my father in the Lord, Pastor Mouelle Marcel, and Suzanne Mouelle of Blessing World Ministry, who led me to Christ and caused me to attend the Bible School of Discipling the Nations Ministries, where I received my miracle testimony.

My thanks to Minister Khalea Queen for her consultation and editorial work in the preparation of this manuscript.

I want to thank Gwendylon Gray- Pompey Mensah for editing this manuscript as well.

Many thanks to Jacinta Kemboi, Chantale Epee, Angeline Pokam, and Jacqueline Nkom for sharing their testimonies with my readers.

Thanks to my Mother Marie—Louise Ngo Yem, for sharing her testimony with my readers and for her encouragement and support.

I want to thank my parents Ngan Nyunai and Agathe Ngan, for their love. Thanks to all my brothers and sisters for making this story possible.

I want to thank my publisher, Roy Kamau & GREAT Books, for helping me into the birth of this magnificent product.

# 1

# My Origins

God protected me even before my salvation: Djoum, my native land.

I was born in Cameroon, Central Africa, in a remote place called Djoum, located in the southern region of Cameroon. After finishing his education, my father moved to Djoum and started working as a biology teacher in the only high school in the area. I do not quite remember my childhood in Djoum; however, I have seen pictures of myself and have somehow tried to connect to the place where I was born later in my life.

I grew up in Yaoundé in a neighborhood called Etoug-Ebe. My father bought a piece of land in that neighborhood and built a house. We were not in faith, but I remember hearing my mom pray "Our Father in Heaven" every morning but never saw her going to church besides for weddings or funerals. Yet, my grandmother had taught me how to pray and go to church. I used to go to church every Sunday with her and made it a habit. I joined several groups in the church, including the choir and a youth group. I had the general notion of God but with no intimacy or relationship with Him.

The relationship with our neighbors was not good at all. Children were fighting, and parents were always quarreling. I remember a time when my mother got sick to the point of becoming psychotic. She went to the hospital, trying to figure out what she was suffering from to no avail. She finally went to a traditional doctor and learned a spell had been cast on her. In Africa, in general, and Cameroon in particular, witchcraft is a reality and can cause a person to get sick. Such illnesses cannot be treated in the hospital. Therefore, people believe they must get protection from a witch doctor to avoid spells, curses, and even setbacks.

There was a time when an old blind man came to our house and spent the night. My parents told us that he came because our neighbors were practicing witchcraft to harm us, and therefore the old blind man with supernatural powers had come to bless and protect our home. The old blind man cooked some meat in banana leaves. When the meat was ready, he called the whole family to come and share the meal. We were eight children and both our parents. The quantity of meat in the banana leaves could only feed two adults, but we all ate the meal until we were full, and the meat in the banana leaves never ran out; it was just supernatural! Till today I don't understand why we were eating that meal, but my parents told us that the old blind man came to protect us.

Moreover, the old blind man took razor blades and made scarifications on our wrists. It was only later that I understood that when you make God the standard for your life and Jesus Christ the center of your life, you don't need to go to any man for protection. When you do so, you dishonor God.

Even though I was not living a holy life, God kept me and protected me. As He said in his word in Acts 17:30, *"God overlooked such ignorance of the past but commands to repent."* God's Grace worked in my life not because of who I was but because of who He is. I gave birth without pain several times, and the spiritual atmosphere in my family when I was growing up cannot justify such a miracle. I could not have inherited such blessings from my mother because she never mentioned giving birth without pain. My mother herself was surprised by what God was doing in my life.

Another example of how God protected me even before my salvation was when I went back to Djoum to collect some critical documents required by the government of Cameroon as part of the hiring process for civil servants. In Cameroon, to be considered for government positions, candidates are required to provide a police report. I went back to Djoum in that context and had the opportunity to reconnect with my native land. As I was preparing for my trip, my father called me to give me directions and instructions.

> He said, "San... Here is the money for your trip. Make sure you keep it dearly. You will take the bus in a neighborhood called Mvan. When you get to the bus area, you will know it is the place because bus drivers' helpers will be calling on customers. They will be saying something like 'a Djoum, a Djoum, a Djoum' to draw the attention of passengers."

My father also advised once I got to Djoum to ask for the residence of the "sous-préfet" (Divisional Officer) so I could spend the night there. He said the "sous-préfet" is there to protect people who are coming from afar. Having received my father's instructions, I left with confidence, knowing that everything would be just fine.

On a Tuesday morning, I said goodbye to my parents, brothers, and sisters and hit the road. When I got to Mvan, just like my father said, the bus drivers' helpers were screaming, *"Djoum, Djoum, a Djoum."* I just followed them, paid the trip fare, and got on the bus. What my father did not tell me was that the trip was very long.

We spent a whole day traveling. We left Yaoundé at 6 am and arrived in Djoum around 10 pm. We had to stop three or four times to ease ourselves or get something to eat. After spending about 16 hours with the same people on the bus, I made some friends. There were a couple of people I was speaking with on our way to Djoum. I even shared my food with one of them. It was not strange because everybody was just so nice and joyful. At no time did I hear anyone complain or be upset about anything. We were not related, but the passengers' attitude towards one another was quite surprising to me.

As we were about to arrive at Djoum, one of the persons I befriended asked me where I was heading. I told him I was going to the "sous- préfet." He then started talking to me with a lot of respect because the "sous-préfet" is respected in such areas as the main administrative authority. Everyone took their belongings when we got off the bus, but I could not find my friend anymore. He was undoubtedly in the crowd somewhere. As I was exhausted, I spotted a bench at a corner and sat there. It was 10 pm. I took the money my father gave me and secured it in my slim jeans. My father had told me to keep my money carefully. No one could reach my money where I hid it in my jeans.

As I was sitting on the bench thinking, I saw a person coming towards me. It was my friend from the bus. I was so relieved and happy to see him.

***"Where is the residency of the sous - préfet?" I asked him.***

He just pointed to it. It was not far from the bus park. He asked me if I was a relative of the "sous préfet," which I answered no.

***"But what are you going to do there at 10 pm?" He said.***

I told him that I came to Djoum for my police report and I needed to leave as soon as I received it because the deadline to apply for my job was approaching.

In Cameroon, when someone is surprised by what you are saying, they will clap their hands as a sign of amazement. That is what he did. He laughed and told me I would not be allowed to the "sous- préfet" residency at that time because it was too late.

I remembered my father's instructions, but my mind was spinning, wondering what I should do. As I asked myself those questions, my friend proposed that I spend the night in his family's house and report to the "sous préfet" first thing in the morning. I found his proposition appealing and then started asking myself a bunch of questions again. What if this, what if that—but I accepted and said to myself that God would protect me. I had already had an experience of the power of God, so I knew what God could do.

Together we went to his house. He knocked at the door, and a woman responded and came over to open it. She gave me a big hug as she was so happy and so welcoming. I was amazed that she was even calling me her daughter. I did not remember that my friend had made any phone calls to announce we were coming, so I was surprised that the lady (my friend's mom apparently) was behaving as if she had been waiting for me; she was so lovely to me. O well!

The lady had cooked, so she served us food, and I ate well since I was starving. After we ate, it was already about midnight; I was getting tired and wanted to sleep.

**Suddenly, the mom said, "alright I will let you go to your place then."**

I was like, are you kidding me? I thought this was the house. So, we had to go somewhere else. We left the house and walked about 10 minutes to my friend's place. It was just a bedroom, so my heart started beating faster. But I was trusting God.

I prayed to God and asked for his protection, but it was too late to go anywhere else anyway; I just had to trust God. I had my slim jeans on with my big leather belt. There was no way those jeans would come off. That was the longest night yet the shortest night of my life. I could not sleep. My father had warned me to keep the money dearly. Not only was I supposed to save the money, but I was also in danger myself.

I slept on the edge of the bed. At some point, my friend went outside for a few minutes, so I adjusted my jeans and belt and re-secured the money in my jeans. When he came back in, he asked me why I was sleeping on the edge of the bed. I did not respond as I was waiting to see what he was about to do.

As I was still thinking, he crawled in the bed. I dared to ask him if he was going to share the bed with me. He said yes. My heart was jumping from my chest to my belly repeatedly. I believe we were sleeping for about two hours when I woke up because I felt somebody touching me. I screamed and threatened him to leave if he repeated that action. He promised not to do it again.

Thirty minutes later, he touched me again, so I left the room. It was 3:00 am. He begged me to come back and said that he did not think I was serious. I came back, slept for an hour, and could not find sleep anymore. I was waiting for the daylight.

At 5:00 am that morning, I was out of that bedroom, amazed that God truly protected me. I went straight to the sous- préfet. They gave me a room, took care of me, and warned me never to retake such risk. After obtaining my police report, I left Djoum with a great feeling. It was indeed my native land. The land that heard my first cry the day I was born. I realized that God's Grace manifested in my life for so long, but I was blind therefore not grateful enough.

Today, as I am under the leadership of my Senior Pastor, I now understand the meaning of Grace. Grace is everything; it is God himself, and there is no life without Grace. The Lord has allowed me to experience His Grace in my life in many ways, especially in my pregnancies and deliveries, by giving birth without pain four times.

# 2

# Labor Pains Are Real

### About My Elder Sister

I grew up in a large family. My mom had eight children, and I always knew that when I got married, I would have children. Having children was one of my dreams, and it became a challenge when I was a teenager. As a teenager, I was a member of a Catholic group called JEC (Jeunesse Estudiantine Chrétienne). We used to organize conferences, seminars, picnics to gather as young people, to learn and fellowship.

There was a time when we held a conference with some Sisters (nuns) of the church. After their presentation, we were allowed to ask questions. I asked a question that the sisters did not like. They found the question provocative and considered that I was demeaning their faith.

Later, one of the nuns came to talk to me and said, *"Look how skinny you are! You can never have children being this skinny."* I felt so bad. I could not imagine myself without children. When she said that, I said to myself, I do not care about what this nun is saying, but God will give me children. What she told me was always in my mind, but I believed in God that what the nun said was not true.

Today I realize that what the nun was saying that day was not from God. The blessing of the Lord was dormant in my life, waiting to manifest in due time.

The negative words of that nun troubled me for a long time but disappeared when my sister got pregnant.

*Maama* is what our entire family called her. She was the oldest of eight children, and therefore she was taking care of all of us, little brothers and sisters. There was a time when my mother started a job outside of the house. Every day she will leave us in the care of Maama. My little brother *Paa* was so used to staying home with my mom that he did not know what to do when she started working. He was looking for her everywhere. He was a toddler and could only say one or two words. Of course, his favorite word was *mama*. Since he was looking for my mother everywhere, he realized that the only person that could earn that name was my elder sister. However, he knew she was not my mother and started calling her *Maama* instead. We all laughed at that but adopted that name for her. She was indeed our little maama. She was doing beyond what a sister would do. She would cook for us, bathe us, wash our clothes, and take us to school.

When we grew up as young adults, Maama started working as a tutor. She was not making much but was using her money to take care of all of us. In Cameroon, it is a custom that the older sibling takes care of the younger ones.

I remember one day when my older brother needed some money that equaled Maama's monthly salary. My sister gave him all her salary that day. I asked myself if I could ever do anything like that. However, what she did that day challenged me and changed my life. I became a different person and decided to copy what I considered so priceless.

From that standpoint, giving became a lifestyle for me. In fact, when I do not give, I feel useless. All this is thanks to my Maama, who was my role model. She was the person I was looking up to. Her pain was my pain, and her joy was my joy. I wanted her to succeed in life. I wanted to look like her because, in my eyes, she looked so beautiful inside and out.

Forgiveness is one specific characteristic that I saw in her. I did not have patience at all but admired that in her. Maama was my hero, and I wanted to know everything she was doing. Looking up to her transformed me into becoming overprotective because I did not want anybody to harm her. When she met her husband, I remember warning him that he should treat her nicely or else he would hear from me.

Then my sister got pregnant. I was so happy for her. She represented hope for me. Above all, I had a strong belief that every good thing that happens to her would happen to me. Therefore, everything that the nun had told me years back faded. The lies of the nun were no longer troubling me. Then I met a man that changed my life forever.

## Maama's Experience Of Labor Pains

My first experience regarding labor pain was when my elder sister got pregnant with her first child. Seeing her in labor was quite scary especially given the fact that nothing seemed to ease her. I remember seeing her husband so powerless, unable to help in any way.

My sister had locked herself up in her bedroom. I could hear her walking up and down, rolling in bed, jumping, stomping, groaning. Anyone who would see her would figure she was in a lot of pain, pain that I could barely describe. She went to the hospital that day but got sent back home because she was not close to being dilated. She suffered for a whole day and a whole night. It was only early in the morning that she eventually gave birth.

Seeing the beautiful baby named Arthur made me forget a bit about what she had gone through. He was my first nephew, and he made me an auntie. Unfortunately, it was not long until a tragedy occurred that brought back the memories of labor pains in my mind.

My father got a phone call at around 11 pm from the hospital. My sister had taken the baby there; he was only 14 months. He was diagnosed with sickle cell and endured the pain of that disease for months. The baby had severe health issues and eventually died. Oh, it was painful!

I remembered the day she was in severe labor pain. I remembered how she went to the hospital thinking she would give birth but got sent back home. The doctor said that she was not even close to being fully dilated. It was only the following morning that she gave birth after being in pain for a whole day and a whole night. Now the baby was dead. My sister and my father came back home with the body of the baby.

My sister was again in severe pain. My father was hurt; my family was grieving. We had just lost a loved one. I was asking myself why a woman would go through the pain of delivery and then go through the pain of grief. Not just any woman, but my sister. Why was childbearing so painful?

> *"To the woman he said: I will make your pains in childbearing very severe: with painful labor, you will give birth to children..." Genesis 3:16*

Indeed, labor pains are real. It is universally known that a woman who is having a baby will be in pain. Labor pains are known to bring the most severe anguish to both the body and the soul. Moreover, childbirth brings sorrow and fear, and the pain is usually associated with punishment. Labor pains can be severe, sharp, or acute. They are compared to afflictions and tribulations in the scriptures.

Scientists, naturalists, and other scholars have managed to find strategies that will lessen the pain of labor. Because almost all women have experienced labor pain, it has become an experience that defines a woman. One of the definitions of a woman in the dictionary refers to an adult human being who is biologically female, capable of bearing offspring. Those who agree with this definition associate their womanhood with their ability to carry a baby in their wombs and deliver them naturally while bearing the worst pain in the universe. Now, women take pride in their pain and get congratulated for bringing life in such a way.

## Overcoming Labor Pains

Because of the pain associated with childbirth, scientists and naturalists have developed ways to ease labor pain. News headlines, journal articles, and papers that allegedly provide solutions to reduce the pains of childbirth are attractive to almost every woman who aims to become pregnant someday.

Titles such as *"Effective Methods To Ease Labor Pain,"* *"Alternative Relaxation*

*Techniques," "Dealing With Pain During Labor"* are very attractive. They attempt to provide women with step-by-step instructions or a recipe that usually does not work because every woman is different, and their bodies manage pain differently.

Non-medication approaches such as walking, breathing exercises, heat packs, or relaxation techniques are said to be helpful to make it a little easier to bear the pain. Scientists invented the epidural, which is said to be very effective and can almost always relieve pain better than any medications or other techniques. Most women who had an epidural felt little to no pain.

During pregnancy, many women reflect on their ability to cope with labor pains during birth. Some of them are brave enough and not ashamed to decide to have an epidural. Others would rather avoid medication and have their baby come naturally.

Most women have made up their minds; they have accepted the pain of childbearing, and they know it is something all women must go through. That seems to be what defines them. However, our God is way greater than what we can imagine, and we cannot limit our understanding of womanhood to painful childbirth.

Women have a greater destiny on earth. We all know the joy and the awesomeness of being a mother, and we should not limit our Great God to doing things only a certain way. Although it is a biological fact that most women experience the pain of labor, it is essential to understand that our God can do anything, even what has never crossed the mind of human beings. Paul said in the Book of Timothy that *"women, however, will be saved through childbearing if they continue in faith, love, and holiness with self-control."* (**1 Timothy 2:15**)

The very day Jesus Christ came to live in you, He moved His headquarters in your heart, and you became the home of extravagant Grace. I honestly never understood what the Grace of God meant, but there was a day the Lord reminded me of what happened in my life. I then realized that my life was the fruit of extravagant Grace. I had a great testimony that I was always thrilled to share because I knew it was not normal. The Bible furthermore implies the power of God through the story of the Hebrew women who were not like the

Egyptians in the Book of Exodus.

## The Midwives and The Hebrew Women

The Book of Exodus in the first chapter mentions a new king who came with new rules and new plans. His ultimate goal was to exterminate the people of Israel, who happened to be mightier than the Egyptians. To put his plan into execution, the new king set taskmasters over the people of Israel.

Their role was to afflict them with their burdens. The Egyptians made the life of the people of Israel miserable. They made their lives bitter with hard bondage, mortar, brick, and all manner of service in the field; all their service, wherein they made them serve, was rigorous. However, the more they afflicted them, the more the people of Israel grew stronger and multiplied. The situation became so uncontrollable that the king had to come up with new ideas. Perhaps he had to go to the source and stop the babies from being born. That is how the midwives became an asset for the king.

Why would midwives appear to be so respected and treated with diligence by the king? What made them so important that they merited to be directly spoken to by Pharaoh himself? The fact that the king broke the protocol and went to talk to the midwives himself demonstrates that the issue was critical.

The Pharaoh of Egypt was the most important and most powerful person in the kingdom. He was the head of the government and the high priest of every temple. How could he go so low, leaving the second most important after him, the Vizier, who had a huge staff of scribes and assistants in his turn?

This part of the Bible demonstrates that the king might have been overwhelmed by what was happening with the people of Israel. For the one they said to be a half-god to lower himself to speak to midwives implies that there was something supernatural happening in the lives of the people of Israel. Perhaps the king was acknowledging the power of the God that the people of Israel served without saying it out loud. Therefore, it was customary for Pharaoh not to question the midwives when they made up the story about how the Hebrew women were not like the Egyptian women but delivered their babies before the midwives came in unto them.

This statement in the Book of Exodus demonstrates the greatness of God, who can do above what we can think or imagine. While the midwives could imagine a story about the Hebrew women giving birth quickly before they arrived, their imagination was nothing compared to what God can do.

For it is written in 1 Corinthians 2:9 *"What no eye has seen, what no ear has heard, and what no human mind has conceived the things God has prepared for those who love him."* I stand and firmly believe that the impossible can happen no matter the circumstances of these Bible verses. The midwives availed themselves, and God used them to save the lives of the baby boys. In the same way, we all can decide to be the vessel that God will use for his glory. I exhort you to avail yourselves so God can use you from glory to glory.

# 3

# A Love Story

## How I Met Him

I accompanied Brigitte, my best friend, to see her boyfriend, Jacques. They were really in love. I admired them, but I was unaware that someone else, Jacques' cousin, was admiring me in the background.

On that day, I remember that a young man was cleaning the same table repeatedly while glancing at me. I ignored him until later when he officially invited me to his place. I knew his little brother and his cousin Jacques since we were going to the same school. He had seen me dance on TV before seeing me face to face.

I was part of a school contest that National Television broadcasted. The day he invited me, he told me, *"I am going to marry you."* I said to myself, *"I think this little boy is crazy. So, people talk about marriage out there; he also has the gut to open his mouth and say so."* I remained quiet with that in mind.

Eventually, we became good friends, and he accepted to be my tutor. He helped me with my homework all the time, and we used that as an opportunity for us to spend time together.

As time went by, I started finding him very attractive, mainly because he was so smart. Back then, he was taking Italian classes and was speaking Italian. That added to his charm. He was a reading machine. He would read a book every week and tell me the story of what he read.

In the beginning, we saw each other on weekends only; we could not hold ourselves anymore and started seeing each other almost every day. We were in love, and we could not stand the absence of each other anymore. He used to do most of the talking; he would talk about our future together, and I would listen.

However, our flirting time did not last because he had to further his education abroad. My love left me to myself, which left my heart was broken. I was not too sure whether I would see him again.

## The Afternoon Of Goodbyes

I remember the first goodbye after I fell in love with my sweetheart. Disappointed, painful are not strong enough words to describe how much my heart bled. As I said goodbye to my sweetheart, I decided to be strong and not sob in front of him. I was shocked into silence, I could not speak, and I thank God he talked the whole time as he knew how to do it.

His mom cooked his favorite dish, knowing that he would miss her food. My plan was really to spend the whole afternoon with him. Unfortunately, it was almost impossible. As soon as I got in his house, two other people got in and took at least two hours of our time. That happened for the rest of the afternoon.

His family gathered, and friends or other family members would come to say goodbye every hour. I was sitting there, and almost everyone looked at me with much pity. I could feel what was in their minds. In addition, even if they had no concerns regarding me, my mind was running errands, and shame was invading my mind every time someone got in.

I could not go to the airport because he was traveling from the city of Douala. He had to catch the bus from a place called Mvan. I remember walking with him to the bus station. As we were getting closer to the bus door, I did not know what to do, whether to give him a kiss or a hug. I kissed him goodbye and whispered, *"bon voyage."* I stood there until the bus left. He sat by the window so he could see me. He timidly waved at me as the bus was fading to disappear.

Somehow, I was able to get a taxi back to my house. My mood had changed, and my brothers and sisters could notice that. No one said anything; I just went straight to my room.

As soon as I laid in my bed, I realized that the only thing I had left was the memories and the pictures we took together. I kept those pictures like a treasure hoping that we shall see again someday. The following week, I visited his family to inquire about him. They told me that they had communicated with him and that he was all right.

I found it so unfair because I could not even speak with my love. He had already written me a letter describing everything from the time we separated at the bus station to when he was writing to me.

## The Love Letters

Oh, how I was waiting for his letters. We had no Internet then or no phones. We had to do with what the world was offering to us then. Writing letters was a common way of communicating. The process was quite long. You had to take your time to handwrite and then send the letter through the Post Office. The letter could take at least two weeks to reach the person and another week to respond. You had no choice but to develop patience.

When he first arrived abroad, I just had to wait until he communicated with me. His family knew where he was and had a way to get a hold of him. I was not a family member yet; therefore, I could not just inquire about his whereabouts. In the eyes of his parents, we were just friends and nothing more, or at least we did not want them to think otherwise. We tried to keep our relationship secret, but we were disturbed by the circumstances. I had no postal address, and therefore the only address he could use at first was his mother's. She used to work for the Post Office and would grab the letters as she returned home.

While waiting for the letter, I did not know what to expect. I had no clue if he had sent the letter or not. All I knew was that he arrived safely. The tons of questions in my mind... 'Was he going to remember to write to me? Was he serious? Was he not going to be so excited about being abroad? What was I putting myself into? Was I going to be disappointed by the guy? Did I make the mistake of falling in love?'

All these questions could only find an answer once I received the letter. He made the promise to send me a letter as soon as he arrived, but I waited and waited. Every day seemed like an eternity.

The first week was indescribable. I would be on the waiting mode at school because I was going to school with his cousin. That same week, I made sure I would see his cousin and greet him; that way, he would deliver it if he happened to have a message for me.

Unfortunately, on the Friday of that week, I went home so disappointed. I said to myself that I would visit them at least to enquire about him. All they told me was that he had arrived safely. I went home that day without any news again. The following week, I kept on hoping that I would receive something to no avail.

It was only after waiting for a whole month that his cousin came to my house one day. I was not expecting his visit at all. He just showed up and handed me the letter that Darling had sent me. I couldn't express my joy out loud. Inside of me, everything was on fire. I wanted him to leave right away for me to read everything about my love finally. He stayed for a good hour which was torture to me.

He was talking with my brother, who happened to be there. I could not abandon my visitor to my brother. At some point, I went to my bedroom, locked the door, and opened the letter as fast as I could to make sure that my love was the one who sent the letter. I read the first line from the envelope, closed it back, and went back to chat with his cousin. Then it was time for him to leave. I saw him a couple of blocks from my house, ran back home as if I was on a race with someone, rushed to my bedroom, opened the door, and locked myself inside.

Now I could enjoy that first letter. At first, I read the letter while standing up. Then sat down to reread the letter. Every word counted and had a deep and strong meaning for me. The way he introduced the letter and the way he signed the letter answered all the questions I had as to if he would disappoint me or not.

When I read these words, *"My Darling, I have arrived safely ...love, your Casimir,"* my heart melted. My love for him grew more and more. I was able to cherish the time we had spent together and was grateful that it had happened. I missed him so much, but I had my consolation, the letter.

Now I had the pictures he had sent along with the letter. I read that first letter over and over until I memorized it. The following day I responded to the letter and sent it to him also. The first experience was challenging, but for the second letter, I already knew what to expect. The first letter he sent me reinforced my trust and my confidence in him.

We communicated through letters for three years, and one day he sent me a letter saying that we should discontinue our relationship. I could not understand why. Although I did not accept his advice later that year, I figured he was right; maybe the relationship was not meant to be. We both decided to live our lives and forget about each other.

A year before his return home, after losing contact for two good years, I remembered him. I decided to send him an email in which I was enquiring about his marital situation. Technology had advanced; we could now communicate through the Internet. The email I sent him rekindled the fire that once was there until he came back to marry me. We came up with quotes that were strengthening us. Such as, *"My love for you will never fade."*

As my senior pastor usually says, spiritual things are voice-activated. All declarations we wrote in our letters happened, and my love came back to marry me.

## A Dream Come True

> *"I came back to marry you," he said!*

On August 31st, 2002, at around 10 pm, I heard a knock at the door—it was him. My parents were sitting in the living room with my brothers and sisters as I told them he was coming home after six years abroad. Everyone wanted to see him because this does not happen often. Boys make promises to girls, but most of them do not keep them.

I had waited all day until nighttime. I went ahead and opened the door to let him in. I jumped on him in front of my parents without fear or shame but with so much joy. I hugged him so tight; I never knew I would see him again. We hugged each other, expressing the love we had for one another.

As we sat, he greeted my parents and chatted a little bit with them. I was in a rush for him to pay attention to ME only. Since it was nighttime, he had to leave, and that was my opportunity to hear from him finally—just the two of us.

We spoke that night until midnight about everything. He told me, "*I came back to marry you.*" I was shaking with joy. I didn't know how to behave. In my mind, I was asking myself tons of questions. "*Was it going to work? Would I be accepted in his family? Would he find a good job in this country?*" His dad never liked me.

One day he told me that I was wasting my time with his son and that he was gone for good and would never come back. Anyway, he was right there in front of me, so I just had to enjoy his presence. But all these questions never stopped me. I said to myself, the guy is brilliant. He ranked first for the years he spent in college. He will find a job.

Regarding his parents, I thought they would have no choice if we decided to get married. I had myself a job, so I thought we would be fine even if he did not find a job right away. I was not a Christian then, but I had faith that things would work in our favor.

# 4

# My Prayer Partner

My fiancé met a coworker who happened to be his supervisor. By the Grace of God, she was a born-again Christian and invited him to attend a Bible school she had participated in years back. She also introduced us to her fiancé as they were about to get married. They invited us to their wedding, then we developed a good relationship and joined their cell group (Bible study group). The husband eventually became our Pastor, and there we were fed spiritually with the word of God.

They both encouraged us to enroll in the bible school led by the missionary, Hal Rahman. My fiancé and I started attending Bible school a month after we got married. The bible school atmosphere was an environment I had never experienced before. People were so excited about the word of God.

We had a variety of classes, including but not limited to Faith, Stewardship, praise and worship, prayer, discipleship, evangelism. The courses we were taking were very practical, and we even had tests and examinations. We went to school every Saturday for the first year. We had just got married and had no children.

During our studies in Bible school, one of the requirements was to pray for one another. The staff of the school had organized a random drawing of names amongst all the bible school students. At the end of the drawing, every student had two prayer partners because you had to draw a name, and someone had to draw your name. Both of my prayer partners played a significant role in my life, but I will focus on the one whom God used to bring the gift of no labor pain in my life.

My prayer partner was a woman of faith. Unfortunately, I don't remember her name or even her face. I would barely recognize her if I saw her again. When we introduced ourselves to each other, all I remember is that she shared her testimony with me and then disappeared. She never came back to Bible school, and I never saw her again. However, what she told me changed my life forever.

I was newly pregnant and was bragging about it to whoever wanted to hear. She was my prayer partner; therefore, I had to give her information about myself, my concerns, my challenges, and my prayer requests as the Bible school staff required. We were also required to share a testimony with our prayer partner. The Bible school teachers advised us that the prayer partner business was not a joke. They shared with us that miracles had happened in the past through prayer partnering. Therefore, I took it seriously.

I was just recently born again and believed everything I was told. When the Bible school teachers spoke about potential miracles with prayer partners, I knew I would not miss it and started expecting a miracle. I shared with my partner that I was just married and that we were expecting a baby.

My biggest challenge, of course, was that it was my first pregnancy, and I did not know what to expect. On the other hand, my prayer partner told me her life story. She had overcome an abusive marriage where she was beaten and abandoned by her husband with kids to take care of. When her husband left, she had no job and did not know how to handle her situation. On top of that, she was pregnant with her last child and begged for food to eat. She said one day the Lord spoke to her and told her that He had heard her cry and that He would wipe away her tears. She said God told her she would deliver her baby safely and without pain, and what the Lord told her came to pass. She had no labor pains and delivered safely. Then she said the Grace that I received from God can be transferred. You can also receive it if you want.

When I heard that testimony, I asked her twice if she was not joking. She said that if I believed, I could also deliver safely with no pain. That day I told her if it happened to her, then it was possible. I received that testimony and started always claiming it. I just knew that it was going to happen, just like she said.

And it came to pass. I delivered Willy safely without pain. Unfortunately, I never saw her again, but I praised God for that divine encounter. You never know who you will meet.

## Lessons From My Prayer Partner

As I analyzed my prayer partner's declaration of faith, I grasped what it meant to *receive the Grace of God*. "To Receive" is an action verb. Receiving such Grace prompts the receiver to do certain things.

We have all offered a gift to a person at least once in our life. Every time you present the gift, the person is free to receive or reject it. The person will then enjoy the gift if they receive it. If the gift is wrapped in a bag, the person will open it, admire it, and use it. This analogy equally applies to the Grace of God.

In the case of my prayer partner, God gifted her with a gift called *"No labor pain."* She took the present with her arms wide open because she needed it. She had already gone through a lot of suffering. She could have decided to reject the gift, but she willingly accepted it and enjoyed it in the end.

The real first valuable gift she had received was the gift of salvation. She was saved by Grace through faith. She was a child of God who had received the good news of Jesus Christ. Then, she developed a relationship with God in prayer, in the meditation of the word of God, listening to preaching that enabled her to hear from God and believe in what God told her.

God gave her a Rhema[1] word, a revelation that she believed strongly in, deepening her intimacy with God. She also knew the power of the confession of the word of God. Therefore, she testified and spoke the word of God until it happened practically. In times of doubt and trouble, my prayer partner would remind God and herself of his promises. She would surround herself with brethren who would lift her in prayer and encourage her.

---

[1] The Greek word rhéma simply means "any spoken word in season."

The Grace of God has been following me since I was younger and has never stopped manifesting. When I went to Bible school, I had no idea that my motherhood would be transformed. I had never heard about a painless birth before until my prayer partner mentioned it in her testimony. I can only attribute this to the Grace of God because I never planned to meet this specific person with such testimony.

I don't know whether my prayer partner was an angel or a regular person. I am sure that she came into my life on a mission to sow a seed. When her mission was fulfilled, she vanished; I never saw her again. It reminds me of the story of Philip and the Ethiopian eunuch in Acts 8:26-39.

The Bible declares that once Philip had baptized the eunuch and he came up out of the water, the Spirit of the Lord carried Philip away, and the eunuch saw him no more and went on his way rejoicing. Similarly, my prayer partner disappeared; I never saw her again, but the words of her testimony caused me to believe in something completely unnatural, mysterious, supernatural. Although I never heard about such things before, I believed it would be awesome to have such an experience. Like the eunuch, I went on rejoicing.

According to my prayer partner, God had spoken to her and promised that she would give birth without pain. She firmly believed in that promise, and it came to pass. Likewise, I believed in it, and it also came to pass.

# 5

# A Cult or a Husband?

> *"The Messiah will find you a husband..."*
>
> *"Oh no, I already have one he is abroad; he is coming soon."*

Before his return, I joined a religious cult where they taught me Jesus had already come. One day in a group session, I requested to see that Jesus. I told the leaders that for me to continue listening to whatever they said, I had to see that Jesus. I knew some basics about the Christian faith.

For example, I knew that God could be everywhere; therefore, asking to see Jesus was not supposed to be a big deal. The church leaders allowed me to meet many other leaders of the organization but not the one they called the messiah. At some point, they told me that only their god, their messiah, would find a spouse for me. They asked me to provide my picture so that the messiah would match me with the person of his choice.

I asked to see the messiah again before I would provide my picture. They got frustrated and asked me why I was difficult. I told them I already had a husband who was outside of the country and was coming soon. I had no clue he was coming back. I had tried to get a hold of him, but I had not contacted him in a long while.

I went back to his parent's house and asked for his contact information. His little sister gave it to me, and that was it. I had broken up with the boyfriend I had then and had decided to be alone and wait for my husband. For two years, I had no relationship with any man until my husband-to-be came back.

My husband-to-be had given his life to Christ years back, and upon his return, he wanted to make sure we were in the same boat. I told him he needed to join my religious cult before we could get married. I was not deeply involved in that religious organization. I had just declined a marriage that the organization was forcing me to get into, so I was just being stubborn and wanted my husband-to-be to join the organization and experience what we were doing. He refused to join the cult and instead decided to pray over it. He said that days after he prayed, I eventually left the cult and accepted to marry him.

## How We Came About The Names Of Our Children

My husband's childhood was quite challenging. His father was violent and abusive with his mother. They often physically fought in front of the children. Since my husband was the oldest son, he would always attempt to stop their fight as early as when he was 14 years old. At times his father would push him away, punch, or even hurt him. He would go on his knees, begging his father to keep the peace at home. The atmosphere in their house was just unbearable. Every day was a day of sadness and sorrow because they never knew what their father would come up with. That situation drew him closer to God. He would lock himself in his bedroom to cry and talk to God.

At 14 years old, while talking to God, he received answers to several questions that he diligently recorded in a journal. One of his prayers to God was that he never wanted to reproduce what he had experienced in his childhood. He dreamt and prayed about having a good marriage and family where a father, mother, and children would live in harmony.

In one of his sessions with God, he received the names of our children. He wrote them in his journal and kept them till he found me. The day he met me, he told me that I brought joy to his life and that he would marry me. Later, he shared the names that he had received with me.

He received Wilfred and Yvan for the boys, and I was convinced about those names in my heart. He had also received names of girls. However, we did not use them because they reminded me of people I knew whose stories were not good.

One of the names reminded me of our spiritual daughter's baby girl who had passed in my husband's car. The other name reminded me of a bad neighbor. We both agreed to name the girls differently. We wanted a girl very badly, so when the first girl came, it was an answer to our prayer, but God had also confirmed His word by allowing me once more to give birth without pain. We were overwhelmed with joy, and therefore, we named our baby Joy. Our last daughter came as the fulfillment of God's Grace in our life, so we named her Grace.

# 6

# My Story of No Labor Pains: The Birth of Willy

*"How will I know that the time has come for me to deliver…"*

*"Oh, you will know it's the time! Your body will speak to you."*

I got pregnant right after our wedding and was due to deliver at the end of May. On May 10th, four days before my birthday, my water broke. I thought I had peed on myself and just went ahead and changed. A couple of minutes later, I had to go back and change again. I then realized something was going on and asked a neighbor about it. I had seen my elder sister in labor when she was about to have her baby. She was in pain. Since I was not feeling any pain, I could not imagine the time had come for me to deliver.

I knocked at my neighbor's door and asked, *"how will I know that I am about to give birth? "She responded: "oooooh, you will know… your body will speak to you."* I said, "ok."

What I understood was that I was going to be in pain. I waited for some minutes, went back to see her, and explained that I had already changed twice because I was wet. She gave me some instructions to follow. She specifically advised me to use a pad and wait.

As soon as I wore the pad, I got wet again and had to change again. This happened several times. She was amazed and said, *"your water broke; you will have a baby. We need to rush to the hospital now."*

My husband was still at work, so I went to the hospital with her. Meanwhile, she called her sister, explaining that she did not understand what was happening because my water broke, but I had no pain. When I realized I was about to have a baby, I overheard her discussing that I seemed to have no pain. I then remembered the testimony I had heard in Bible school at the early stage of my pregnancy.

> *"What are you here for?" The patient in labor asked me.*
>
> *"To have a baby," I replied.*
>
> *"And you look like this?" bewildered in disbelief.*

As I remembered the testimony of my prayer partner that day, I also remembered that as a born-again Christian, I was a new creation. Old things had passed. For that reason, God, the one who lived in my heart, could do anything, even enable me to give birth without pain. I was a bit scared but strongly believed that it would happen.

When I got to the hospital, several women were already admitted, and some of them were screaming at the top of their lungs in painful labor. One of them asked me, *"what are you here for?"* I said, "to have a baby." She replied, "and you are like this?" She returned to her screaming.

The midwife was… a guy. He asked me how I knew that I was having a baby because I did not look like somebody who was about to have one. I told him what happened that day, then he checked me and admitted me.

I was sharing a room with other women who were waiting to give birth. I could tell that some of them were in excruciating labor. I was lying in my bed, patiently waiting for the baby to announce itself. I was chatting with Angel, the lady who took me to the hospital (my neighbor).

At some point, she approached the nurse to ask her for something. I remember that she asked me for some money that she was going to give to the nurse. According to their assessment, the money was intended to buy some pills that would help accelerate labor since I was not in labor. I just gave her the money as I did not quite understand what was going on.

Later, she returned with a suppository and instructed me to wear it, saying it would help me start the actual labor. I went to the bathroom and wore it. An hour later, I was sitting there chatting with her. Occasionally, she would ask me if I felt some pain, and I would say no. I realized she became more worried every time I responded no.

*"San, do you feel some little pain?" The nurse asked.*

*"Ummmm, NO."*

Angel was going back and forth in my bedroom to check on me. She was checking to make sure the labor had started. The nurse installed a monitor to check the baby's heartbeat and see how my contractions were evolving. I was in labor, but I could not feel anything at all.

My husband arrived at the hospital, and Angel told him what was going on. He, too, became worried. When they both came into my room to check on me, I saw on their face that they were worried. I realized that telling them I was not feeling anything would worry them more, so I told them what I knew they wanted to hear to ease their minds.

When Angel asked again if I was feeling some pain, I said yes. When my husband asked the same question, I told him I was feeling some pain. He felt relieved! Angel told the nurse I had started to feel some pain. They waited for a little while since I was still awake chatting with them. Then the nurse asked Angel to convince me to get some rest and that if I slept, they would know for sure that I was not feeling anything. I laid down and slept until the morning. They realized I had no pain at all.

The following morning, because my water had broken the night before, the doctor said they would speed up the labor process. They gave me a suppository. Other women in the room received the same. The woman who was lying beside me started screaming immediately after. Another one started screaming a couple of minutes later. These two women gave birth 3 to 4 hours later after being in so much pain. My case, however, was different. I was still the same; the "magic" suppository did not work in my body. I had no pain.

At some point, the doctor told me that I might have a C-section if I did not go into labor. Before then, they placed me on an IV infusion. While on that infusion, I started feeling cramps like I was on my period. I was also sweating a lot. That was how I gave birth to Willy.

I realized that what my prayer partner said had happened. Everyone was amazed at what happened in my life with the birth of Willy. I praise God for his abundant Grace. To hear and to be blessed! I saw it with my own eyes. The Lord blessed me with a pain-free delivery. I said to myself, *"this shall happen with all my deliveries!"*

# 7

# The Birth of Yvan

> *"Please do not do this to me... do not give birth at home... I beg you in the name of God!"*

My husband got a new job and was assigned to a remote area when I became pregnant for our 2nd child. Knowing what had happened with our first child, we figured that it was safer for me to stay in a big city where we could find good hospitals. As he went to his assignment, I moved to my pastor's house since I was almost due. We didn't want to take the risk of going far from the city.

On one fateful night, a sister I used to call *Mama Chantou* cooked some types of veggies with grounded yams. I ate that food a lot and went to bed around 10 pm. I was ready to have the baby; I knew I could have him anytime. I went to bed and had a dream of a lady that was amazed at something she saw and said, "I can't believe this is how women give birth. It is so fast! Just like in the Bible."

Upon waking, I felt a growing rush in my bladder as I raced to the toilet. However, my relief from emptying my bladder grew to worry as the flow surprisingly wasn't ending. I tried to stand up but I couldn't. Something was holding me down as if I had a big load in my lower back. I had to stand up to go back to sleep. Nevertheless, I forced myself to stand up and hit the hallway. As I was heading to my room, a gush of water spilled on the floor; my water had broken.

I rushed to the room, woke up Mama Chantou, with whom I was sharing the room. I suggested she get ready for the hospital. She was still sleepy, so my statement was somehow shocking to her. As she was listening, another gush of water hit the floor in front of her.

> *She was afraid and started saying "please, please don't do this to me! What am I going to do? What will I tell your husband, please I beg you."*

She was panicking and shaking; her attitude made me laugh so bad. I couldn't stop laughing at her. I kept on telling her that I was fine, but she was so scared. She then rushed to our pastor's room, knocked at his door but surprisingly, found it opened.

> *She got in the room, tapped his feet, and said, "Brother Marcel, Brother Marcel, Sandrine is about to have the baby, let's go to the hospital!"*

Mama Chantou came back into the room and told me what happened when she woke the pastor up. She described what the pastor did and how he jumped off his bed when he heard that I would have the baby. Mama Chantou was not a petite woman; she was quite heavy yet beautiful. Seeing her jump to mimic what she saw was quite funny. I laughed hysterically. As I was laughing, another gush of water was on the floor. The baby was heading down; I could feel him going down. He was pressing down every time I laughed.

Mama Chantou was not stopping! I couldn't stop laughing either, and my laugh was pushing the baby down.

> *Mama Chantou was saying things such as, "you want to give birth in the car... Oh my God... what am I going to do? Sandrine you have killed me!"*

Everything was just too funny for me. I couldn't stop laughing. Meanwhile, the baby was coming. I had no pain at all, not even the cramps I had with Willy.

Nothing!

When I say extravagant Grace, it is beyond belief. It doesn't make any sense at all. How could this happen? The Love of God was indescribable. None of my words can ever describe this type of Grace. Why me? How did it happen?

I didn't even know how to pray; I was born again for about three years only. I never liked fasting; I was not the nicest person; instead, people said I was mean. I had left my past life only a few years earlier. How could God forget so soon and grant me this type of Grace? Grace truly means unmerited favor. This was the perfect example of God's love for his children. The blood of Jesus had completely washed all my sins away, and He made me whole. Jesus himself moved his headquarters into my heart. Grace herself lived in me and manifested through me.

## The Longest Yet Funniest Trip of My Life

Traveling in Cameroon can be very challenging due to the condition of both the roads and the cars. Traveling within the city requires using your car or taxis and motorbikes, which are public transportation. Motorbikes, though dangerous, are quite faster because their sizes allow them to find their way in-between cars even in traffic jams easily. Because there are no consistent road safety rules, many accidents occur every day, putting both motorists' and pedestrians' lives at risk. Moreover, the roads are poorly maintained hence not safe to operate on. There are few roads, little-to-no traffic signs, and speed limits are neither posted nor enforced.

In Cameroon, you can either use a shared taxi or taxi drop. You must stand on the roadside and yell at the driver to indicate your destination and the price you are ready to pay. If the driver goes in the same direction, they will stop and take you. Prices depend on the distance.

Usually, taxis take up to five passengers. Taxi drop is more private and allows flexibility. You can be by yourself in the taxi or ride with your family or friends. This method of transportation is more expensive, especially at night. You might be asking yourself why I describe the roads of Cameroon, but this is because they played a significant role in the delivery of my second child.

In the city of Douala, my pastor lived in the *Bonakouamouang* neighborhood, right by CETIC Akwa after the roundabout. The gate of the house was near the main street of that area. You could hear cars honking and people walking and talking on the street. The area was quite busy and noisy. It was around midnight when my pastor, Brother Marcel, got out in front of the gate searching for a cab. In Cameroon, you don't call for a cab on the phone; you trust God that a taxi driver will pass near you and drive in the direction you want to go.

On average, a taxi ride costs about 200 CFAF for a short distance, which equals about 50 cents. We headed to the Douala General Hospital, about 9 kilometers away, but the roads were terrible. Due to the urgency of the situation, we had to catch a taxi drop to be the only ones riding in it.

After waiting for about 10 minutes, Brother Marcel got a taxi and called us. Mama Chantou and I jumped in the car, and the longest and funniest trip started. As I mentioned earlier, the condition of the roads is poor. Therefore, for someone who is about to give birth, riding a car is not pleasant.

I could feel every move the car made. It was like when you were in a bouncy house. Before you finish processing the previous bounce and bump, the next one has started. I could get some rest from bouncing every five minutes. The roads had big potholes, and they were not paved. The shortest distance seemed the longest because you didn't know what to expect and when the next bump would come. The driver had to drive gently and be extremely cautious to avoid damaging his car and hurting the passengers. There was quite nothing the driver could do to help. That is just the way the roads are. It was not his fault if I was having a baby and already giving birth. I would have been more comfortable walking than riding the cab, but I had no choice.

Every time the car moved, I could feel the baby jumping up in my belly and then pressing down. I couldn't keep quiet when I was feeling the pressure. I was so afraid of the possibility of giving birth in the car. Every time I told Mama Chantou that the baby was pressing, she would complain, scream, cry, and talk. She was going through all types of emotions. The way she was expressing her emotions was so funny to me. I would say that she was in labor for me while I was having fun laughing at her. You should have seen her face and her moves. Every time she moved, I would burst out laughing, which pushed the baby down some more. I thought the baby was going to be born in that car. My water had broken at home, and as the baby was pressing down, the water kept coming out. The back seat was all wet even though I had put a towel on my seat.

The driver never looked back at us until we arrived at the hospital. My pastor was sitting in the passenger seat; I was in the back seat with Mama Chantou. I was sitting behind the pastor while Mama Chantou was behind the driver. I was trying to make the conversation at some point in the car, but it was not possible.

Mama Chantou was scared; she was complaining and shouting. She was so agitated. Meanwhile, the pastor and the driver were the quietest people on earth. The pastor never spoke to me about his experience that day. I can guess what was going on in his mind. Maybe he was praying the whole time, interceding. We had already lost a member of the church as she was giving birth. A couple of months earlier, a member of the church did not make it during delivery. She had a lot of complications, and both she and the baby died. It was a disaster in the church. The pastor was discouraged; he was called names, heavily criticized, and laughed at.

As I remembered that incident, I thought that the pastor could only be praying, casting out all demons that could take my life and that of the baby. But I was sitting by Mama Chantou. She couldn't stop!

What made me laugh the most was that she was more concerned about what people would say. I kept asking myself what she was thinking. Now I understand that she thought I was going to die since I had no signs of pain. My water broke at home, and usually, that's about the time when labor pain is at its peak. But I had none. What else could it be in her mind if not that I was giving up on my life and letting myself die?

**"Why didn't you come earlier?"**

> *"I came immediately after my water broke..."*
>
> *"LIAR!"*

When we arrived at the hospital at about 1 am, I rang the delivery area bell; a midwife opened the door with sleepy eyes. As I got into the area, she closed the door and followed me. I was walking in front of her.

At some point, she passed by me and asked me where the person who rang the doorbell was. I told her that it was me. She replied that she meant the lady who was going to have the baby. I repeated that it was me. She asked me how I knew; I then told her that it was because my water had broken. She looked at me like, why did you even wake me up? You cannot be having a baby and looking like this. She carelessly told me to lie down on a bed so she could check me.

I laid down, and when she came to check me, she screamed on top of her lungs and started yelling and calling out for help. She even asked me where my mom was with the towels and everything else. She called two other nurses. Her agitation was further making me laugh. In my heart, I was like, good for you! Next time you will listen when I talk.

She asked me why I didn't come earlier. I told her that my water had broken, and we arrived immediately. She didn't believe a word I said and called me a liar.

> **She started yelling at me saying, "you... these young ladies... you wanted to kill that baby... why did you wait? The baby is here, I can see his head."**

She then realized that I was not in pain; I had no signs of labor, but the baby was heading out. She got scared and started calling me. Madam, are you ok? She started screaming out of fear. She said things such as, "*what is this? Help! I have never seen this....*"

She asked one of the nurses to bring an IV infusion. Meanwhile, she started pressing on my belly, asking me if I could feel her. I looked at her and asked her back if she wouldn't feel it if I started pinching her. She got more scared.

> *I furthermore told her, "Ma'am, there is no need to be scared. This is how I had my first son. I give birth without pain."*
>
> *She looked at me and responded, "what do you know about pregnancies? Talking nonsense."*

As she was talking, the other nurse came in with the infusion. I asked her what the infusion was for; she didn't even listen to me. I kept on asking why she wanted to install that infusion on me, what the purpose was. As she tried to put it on my arm, the other nurse called her to help me deliver the baby. Two minutes before Yvan was born, I felt like he was fighting inside me, trying to find his way out. I just had to push once, and that was it. He was out.

By the Grace of God, Yvan was born so fast. I never felt any pain AT ALL. Yes, I had heard what had happened to my partner once; I had experienced it with my first son. I had seen it, it was real, and I was experiencing it with my second son.

Now, I genuinely believe anything is possible with God. It does not depend on me, but it depends on the Grace of God. All I must do is embrace that Grace and receive all the benefits attached to it.

## There is Something About Laughing

As I was retracing the memory of how I gave birth to Yvan, I remembered one specific detail—the fact that I was laughing throughout labor until I had him. There is something good that comes out of laughter.

Several authors conducted a research study about laughter and humor. Commonly known, laughter is good medicine that helps people to be relieved. Their study explored what laughter is and its effects based on scientific and psychological research.

Laughter is a language understood by all human beings in the universe, unlike people's common languages. Laughter is not learned; as a matter of fact, it begins at a very tender age. Laughter is unconscious but can be triggered by an exterior act. It provides powerful, uncensored insights into our unconscious. It simply sprays up from within us during specific situations. When we laugh, we change our facial expressions and produce resonances. During cheerful laughter, the muscles of the arms, legs, and trunk are involved. Laughter also requires modification in our pattern of breathing.

Psychological and social research has demonstrated that laughter plays a role in the reduction of pain. Rosemary Cogan, Ph.D., a professor of psychology at Texas Tech University, discovered that individuals who laughed at a Lily Tomlin video or underwent a relaxation procedure tolerated more discomfort than others.

Another researcher concluded that humor might help temper intense pain. James Rotton, Ph.D. of Florida International University, reported that orthopedic surgery patients who watched comedy videos requested fewer aspirin and tranquilizers than those who viewed dramas. Humor may also help to cope with stress.

In a study by Michelle Newman, Ph.D., an assistant professor of psychology at Penn State University, subjects viewed a film about three grisly accidents and had to narrate it either in a humorous or serious style. Those who used the humorous tone had the lowest negative affect and tension. [2]

All this research shows that laughter is beneficial. It is believed to have the potential to release endorphin and an effect like antidepressants. It is not clear from research how long the result of laughter sticks around, but the burst of brain activity laughing triggers is undoubtedly powerful, at least for a short period.

Laughter could affect somebody as antidepressants do. It activates the release of the neurotransmitter serotonin, the same brain chemical affected by the most common types of antidepressants. No wonder why they say

---

[2] "The Science Of Laughter". 2021. *Psychology Today*. https://www.psychologytoday.com/us/articles/200011/the-science-laughter.

laughter is medicine. Dr. William Strean, a Canadian doctor, wrote an article describing the benefits of laughter. According to him, laughter contributes to the relief of pain. The scientific allegation of laughter matches the significant consideration that God has about laughter. During my second pregnancy, I understood that our God wanted to communicate something great about laughter to me.

Laughter has a communicative power in the bible. It sometimes teases, mocks, or disdains, ridicules, scoffs. (Genesis 21:9; 38:23; 39:14, 17; 2 Chronicles 30:10; Psalm 52:6; 80:6; Proverbs 1:26; Ezekiel 23:32; Habakkuk 1:10). A fool's laughter reveals his folly (Proverbs 29:9; Ecclesiastes 7:6), while the laughter of the righteous indicates confidence in God (Psalm 52:6).

The most significant is God's laughter. The God who created the universe and made me in His image, and from whom I get my laughter. No wonder scientists acknowledge laughter as a distinguishing feature in human beings that comes with many benefits, although little research is published about it.

The scripture tells us that *"God who seats in Heaven Laughs!"* (Psalm 2:4) If Jesus, seated on the throne with God, laughs, and the same Jesus lives in me, why won't He laugh through me? He made me a witness.

He said, *"you shall be My witnesses in Jerusalem, Judea, Samaria, and to the uttermost parts of the world."* (Acts 1:8) Meaning that He would use me, and all I am must reflect who He is: His wonders, His greatness, His magnitude, His miracles, His omnipresence, and omnipotence. If I was laughing while getting ready to give birth to Yvan, it was God Himself who was laughing at and for something.

God's laughter causes demons to tremble. His enemies cringe in fear while his friends rise in comfort. Moreover, his laughter warns the devil and his agents of their imminent doom while reminding saints of their greatness. God laughs at the wicked, for he sees that his day is coming (Psalm 37:12–13).

God laughs at those who set themselves against His anointed (Psalm 59:8). He laughs to give signs to both His enemies and His friends—terrifying signs for His enemies and uplifting signs for His friends. God's laughter gives great comfort to those who love Him. God laughs to dispel our fears. God laughs to remind us of the promise we have received from Him.

From glory to glory, wonder upon wonder, undeserving as we are, He has set his favor on us in His Son Jesus Christ. God laughs at the enemy who thought He won and succeeded in condemning women to labor pain. He laughs at the devil, who is confused by the blood of Jesus. He moreover laughs at the devil who will face judgment forever. God laughs while sitting on His throne.

God laughs for joy, everlasting joy, victory over the devil, pain, sorrow, and sadness. God laughs at the swell of the machinations of the enemy, which are soon overpowered by the happiest and most soothing sound in the universe, resounding down from heaven itself: the monumental mirth of God in righteous laughter.

"*He who sits in the heavens laughs*" (Psalm 2:4). "*God has a smile on His face*" (Psalm 42:5) and fills our mouth with laughter, and our tongue with shouts of joy; then it causes others to say among the nations that the Lord has done great things for them (Psalm 126:2). Indeed, the Grace of God overwhelmed me, granting me a pain-free delivery in laughter.

# 8

# The Birth of Joy

*"You will have a cesarean section... Placenta Previa..." my doctor said.*

*"My God, this was not in our contract," I whispered internally to God.*

In November 2008, when Yvan was 18 months, we moved to the USA in Superior, Wisconsin. We started a new life in a new environment, adjusting to the culture, the language, and the change. We had to start our lives over and find jobs that would allow us to survive in our new country.

Two years later, I was pregnant again. I believed in God for a girl who would have a lot of hair. By the Grace of God, He heard my prayer, and I found out I would have a girl. We decided to name her Joy Laetitia. Which means *JOY JOY*. It was a double joy because God heard my prayer, and I delivered her safely.

I went home that night after the ultrasound and after receiving the diagnosis of my doctor. She said my placenta was coming before the baby, and therefore I could not deliver vaginally. I would have to go through a cesarean section. Moreover, they were going to admit me early not to take the risk of letting me go into labor. If I went into labor, I might bleed to death.

After this diagnosis, they switched my doctor and gave me a specialist in '*at-risk pregnancies.*' On my next appointment, I had to do the last ultrasound that would confirm surgery. Before that day, I decided to talk to God about the situation. I did not sleep that night but sat in my bed to talk to my God.

> ***These are the words I specifically said, "God, this was not in our contract. You told me that I was going to give birth without pain. How can they cut my belly without me feeling some pain?"***
>
> ***I furthermore told him, "I don't want to have a cesarean section."***

Immediately after I said that prayer, I felt things moving in my belly and going back in place. I could feel the baby moving and something going from the bottom to the top. When my husband woke up, I told him that everything was back to normal and that my placenta went back to wherever it was supposed to be. He was in awe but didn't say anything.

That morning was my last scheduled ultrasound before they would have to schedule the caesarean section. I knew the Lord had changed everything in my belly. I knew that He did not lie to me but that He always kept His promises. He promised me I would give birth without pain and never said I would have a caesarean section. That day, I went to the hospital, trusting God that the ultrasound would show something completely different from the doctors' diagnosis.

> ***"Go and wait for the big day... everything is normal."***

I drove to the hospital, parked my car, and climbed the stairs to the scanning area. I announced myself, and they called me later in the room for the ultrasound. The lady who was performing the ultrasound was quite old. To me, she looked like she had quite a good experience and knew what she was doing.

I laid in that bed, and she poured a warm liquid on top of my belly. I observed as she checked all the parts of my belly. Her face was changing every time she touched one part. I could understand through her attitude that the unexpected had happened.

At some point, she asked me again what my name and my date of birth were. I believe that she wanted to make sure she was not dealing with the wrong patient. I gave her my name. She asked me again why I was there. I knew where she was going, but I just replied that they said I would have a cesarean section. She went and rechecked my paperwork and came back.

She then decided to use another method to perform the ultrasound. She was trying to remain calm, but it was apparent that she was disturbed. She was shocked by what she saw compared to the diagnosis. She started talking to herself, saying things such as, *"what is going on? I don't understand."*

I knew that God had performed a miracle in my life again. At some point, I asked her what was happening? She never responded. Instead, she told me to get dressed and wait for the doctor. As I was waiting for the doctor, I was reflecting on the lyrics of the song I was going to sing in my head and how I would tell that testimony over and over. I was filled with joy. My God had done it again.

> **When the doctor came, she said, "Sandrine, everything is fine and normal, just go home and wait for the big day."**
>
> **I asked the doctor if she was no longer scheduling the cesarean section. She responded, "what for?? You don't need one!"**
>
> **"You cannot have the baby now... it's too early. You need to go back home."**
>
> **"No, I am not leaving this place until I give birth."**

On March 12th, around 6 pm, I went to use the bathroom to ease myself. I realized that there was a pinkish color showing in my undergarment. I said to myself that the time had come to deliver the baby. I spoke to my husband, and he immediately called a couple from our church who volunteered to stay with Willy and Yvan when I would be in the hospital. They came over to our house and picked up the kids.

My husband and I drove to another friend's house who owned an expensive camera as we wanted to use it to take pictures of the newborn. I remember that Jacinta, our young friend, was so surprised. She kept on asking if I was telling the truth that I would have a baby in a little while. What was surprising was that I was comfortable, never seemed in pain, and taking the time to drive to her house for the camera was quite surprising for a woman who was about to give birth.

My husband and I arrived at the hospital and got admitted. A doctor came to enquire about the reason for the visit. Since I was not in pain, he figured that I was not ready to have the baby. He said that I should go back home and come back later or the next day. I boldly told him that I had come to deliver that day and was not going home until I had the baby.

After taking all the details he needed, he left the room and came back later with another doctor. I was still not in pain, so it was not alerting anybody. When the new doctor came over, she checked me and realized that I was 4cm dilated. Since I was not in pain, they thought I was going to be there longer.

A lady from my workplace, a doula, had volunteered to assist me during labor and delivery. She was teaching me breathing techniques for when the time would come to push. She was in the delivery room with my husband and the healthcare practitioners. About 5 to 15 minutes before Joy was born, I felt a sharp pain in my lower abdomen. I had never felt anything like that before.

The pain was like somebody was using a knife inside of me, turning it round to find something, and every time he turned the knife inside, it would cut one part. I don't know how I can describe the pain I felt for maybe 30 seconds. When I felt that pain, I never knew what it was since I never had pain with my deliveries.

I called the nurse and described to her what I just felt. She looked at me like, *is this woman ok? She is here to have a baby, right? Doesn't she know that it hurts?* You could tell what was going on in her mind. She asked me if it was my first baby and that it would hurt, but I told her that I never felt anything with the other ones. I then asked for the doctor and requested an epidural. I told them that I did not want to feel what I felt again, the pain I felt a couple of minutes ago. When the doctor came to check on me, the baby was already heading out, so she said it was too late for an epidural. Joy was born right after that. It was an incredible feeling; I had my girl, and she had a lot of hair, exactly what I had asked God.

I knew that God had answered my prayer. The nurse came over to see me at some point and told me that everyone was looking at the baby with a lot of hair. People were amazed at how much hair the newborn had. It was a testimony, and another prayer answered. As far as the pain was concerned, I realized how much the Lord had blessed me.

I experienced pain for a few seconds only before the delivery. Those 30 seconds of pain felt like forever to me that day. But I have heard testimonies of women who even die because they could not bear the pain of labor, or other women who are in labor for one, two days, or more.

The Grace of God is truly unmerited. God can and will grant you a particular favor not because of you but because of Himself. God loves you and me so much that we cannot find words to describe His love. He can do the things that your imagination would never imagine. God has poured his overwhelming, abundant, extravagant grace on me. He will do so for you too. The Scriptures say that he is unchangeable, the same yesterday, today, and forever. I believe that God wanted me to appreciate the Grace of God better and keep tapping into it. I delivered Joy safely with no labor pains.

God did it again.

# 9

# The Birth of Grace

*"You had a miscarriage."*

I was so happy that I finally had my girl. Joy was born, and I used to call her my mini-me. I had so much fun dressing her up. I enjoyed seeing her as she looked like a little woman. Thank you, Jesus!

Two years later, I thought I was pregnant again and went to see the doctor. They checked me and scheduled an ultrasound since I was bleeding. The ultrasound showed that I was pregnant but had a miscarriage and therefore had to go through a D&C or curettage.

The doctor scheduled the surgical operation for Thursday morning. I was advised not to eat before the surgery. I was supposed to remain on that diet from 10 pm till 10 am of the following morning. You know it is sometimes difficult to keep up when they give you instructions. For some reason, human beings do not like laws; the flesh does not handle being told what to do. Therefore, every time an instruction is given, the flesh wants to rebel against it, and it makes your soul feel bad and makes the situation difficult to handle.

*"I am going to perform a curettage."*

The Lord helped me to be still. I remained still the whole time. As the procedure was approaching, I couldn't find sleep that Wednesday. On Thursday, early in the morning, I told my husband that I was convinced that I should not go through with the surgery. I didn't tell him why. He was just shocked but supported me in the decision I was making. He was a little bit concerned, though, but he had already experienced similar things with me. I thank God for such a supportive husband. He is a blessing.

As I mentioned earlier, I was bleeding all this time, so it was quite alarming. I told my husband that I would look at it as my period. I then called my doctor to cancel the surgery with no explanation. Later that day, I realized that the bleeding had stopped. What had happened? How come I had stopped bleeding suddenly after canceling the surgery?

Six weeks later, I was pregnant with Grace. I went back to see the same doctor. He asked me why I was there; I told him that I believed I was pregnant. He checked me, did the pregnancy test, and confirmed that I was pregnant. This is where the journey of Grace Started.

***"I will call her Grace...."***

As I continue the journey of Christianity, I know I am not just an ordinary Christian. I understand that God has chosen me and has set me apart for his pleasure. Who can forget the nasty things you did if not a loving and caring Father? After living a life that did not glorify God, He still forgave me and washed away my sins forever. God Himself made me whole; He justified me and made me Holy. Now I am a Holy Nation, no longer condemned because Grace has removed the wrath of God through Christ Jesus. The Lord has practically forgotten every single sin I committed and has granted me His extravagant Grace. The type of Grace that almost seems to be wasted.

After giving birth to my first three children, Willy, Joy, and Yvan, I understood that God keeps his promises because He is not a man to lie. The God who spoke to me through a prayer partner and told me that I would deliver without pain did not lie, despite what I had done in the past. That same God made it happen. On my side, it was effortless. Not by might, nor by power, but by my spirit says the Lord. I did not do anything to merit this ultimate favor of God. I just believed and received. I was wondering what would happen with my next child. My God would do that again and again because it is His nature.

When I got the confirmation that I would have a girl, I decided to call her Grace. She represents the fulfillment of God's promise. It is the essence of Christianity. A Christian life aside from Grace is lifeless. Grace made me understand what God had done throughout my life.

By the Grace of God, my mom came over to assist me. She helped with the kids, cooking, and doing housework every single day. She even did my laundry and her grandchildren's as well. I am blessed to have her by my side. My mom would check on me every other hour to ensure that I was fine. We attended a great church, Saint John Baptist Church, in Painesville, Ohio, where God gave us a family. All the members of the church loved us so much.

One grandpa decided to adopt my children. Deacon Jones asked me once if he could adopt my children. I couldn't resist a great person with such a great heart since he had shown so much love to my kids before. He became like my dad in Ohio. Therefore, he knew my due date and had the details of the progress of the pregnancy. He had planned to accompany me to the hospital when the time would come.

My husband got a job opportunity in Maryland. Therefore, he had to leave because he was starting his new job in May. He drove back and forth every other weekend. I was trusting God that he would be around when I gave birth in June.

When I told the story of my pregnancies to my gynecologist about not experiencing the signs of labor, he decided to admit me before the due date. Dr. Ahuja of Cleveland said he would not take any risk. Moreover, he said that I was at risk of giving birth at home if he did not act. My mom already knew how I usually give birth, but she was scared.

One night, I asked her why she was so scared; she explained that she would not know who to call. She was more concerned about the language barrier because, at that time, she did not speak any English. I used to work as a consecutive interpreter from home. She would hear me interpret occasionally. I trained my mom on what to say If my water broke and how to call 911. The idea of calling 911 was just too much for her. She did not like it at all.

The day before my admission to the hospital, my mom cooked so well, but I couldn't eat. I was feeling very weird. I was not comfortable. My mood had changed, and she noticed. At some point, I got a runny stomach and started going to the bathroom every 15 to 20 minutes. My mom suggested that we go to the hospital because she thought I was in labor. Since I couldn't feel any pain, she thought the diarrhea was a sign. I refused to go and told her that the diarrhea was due to some food I had eaten the day before. She got more concerned because she was the cook. Sometime that evening, I felt better and was trusting God that my water would not break overnight.

## Oooh, That's a Big One!

The following morning, we went to the hospital with my mom and Deacon Jones. They installed the monitor on me when we arrived there and realized that I was already in labor. The monitor could show the patterns of labor. The nurse who was with me was looking closely at the monitor when she saw a big contraction.

She looked at me, but I was chatting with my mom and laughing about something.

> *"Oooh, that is a big one! Did you feel it?" her eyes grew wide as she watched the monitor.*
>
> *"What?" I asked.*
>
> *"A contraction." She said.*
>
> *"Where is it?" I held back my smile knowing that she wouldn't understand.*

She gave me that look. When another one came, she turned the monitor and showed me the graph, asking me if I could feel something. I just told her that I never felt anything before and was not expecting to feel anything. She was amazed at what she saw. I was a weird patient. No one, not even the doctor, could understand.

The doctor was glad he admitted me before my due date. As he had said, I could have given birth at home. It was such a wonderful experience. I gave birth the fourth time without pain again!!! What an overwhelming experience!

As I was in my bed holding the baby, I was thinking about all my other kids, Willy, Yvan, and Joy, one after the other. The Lord had been so faithful! He had kept His promise. What a wonderful God we serve! The experiences I had were different with every single child, but the bottom line is that I do not know the pain of labor. Not because I did something big enough to deserve such a gift, but ONLY because of the power of God's Amazing Grace.

# 10

# Conclusion - Lessons From My Story

### The Nature of God: Grace Manifested on Ordinary People

2 Timothy 1:9 sheds some valuable light on the topic of Grace *"he has saved us and called us to a Holy life not because of anything we have done but because of his purpose and Grace. This Grace was given to us in Christ Jesus before the beginning of time."* God's Grace is the foundation upon which the Gospel message is built. That Grace explains the impact and accomplishments that all men of God have achieved.

In His great nature of love, God has demonstrated over the years how much He is indescribable. As believers, we have only experienced a glimpse of who He is. It would be a lie to believe that God, in His immensity, can be understood. The books, the preaching, the testimonies of great men of God, and overall, the Bible, have shown that humankind cannot contain or define the infinite God.

The Grace of God has no limit and can manifest in ordinary people. The examples of Mary, the mother of Jesus, Esther, and Paul will help us understand how God operates with people who are just like you and me.

> *In the sixth month the angel Gabriel was sent from God to a city of Galilee named Nazareth, to a virgin betrothed to a man whose name*

> *was Joseph, of the house of David. And the virgin's name was Mary. And he came to her and said, "Greetings, O favored one, the Lord is with you!" But she was greatly troubled at the saying and tried to discern what sort of greeting this might be. And the angel said to her, "Do not be afraid, Mary, for you have found favor with God. And behold, you will conceive in your womb and bear a son, and you shall call his name Jesus. He will be great and will be called the Son of the Most High. And the Lord God will give to him the throne of his father David, and he will reign over the house of Jacob forever, and of his kingdom there will be no end."*
>
> *And Mary said to the angel, "How will this be, since I am a virgin?"*
>
> *And the angel answered her, "The Holy Spirit will come upon you, and the power of the Most High will overshadow you; therefore the child to be born will be called holy—the Son of God. And behold, your relative Elizabeth in her old age has also conceived a son, and this is the sixth month with her who was called barren. For nothing will be impossible with God." And Mary said, "Behold, I am the servant of the Lord; let it be to me according to your word." And the angel departed from her." Luke 1:26-38*

The Book of Luke in the first chapter narrates the story of a young virgin woman betrothed to Joseph. Mary was engaged and about to get married to her fiancé, Joseph, when she had a visitation from Gabriel, the angel of God. The Bible does not describe any specific criteria that distinguished Mary from other young women of her time.

While we cannot deny the omniscient God who knows the end even before the beginning, the One who might have chosen Mary for reasons we ignore, we still cannot conclude that Mary was exceptional. Mary was young, just like her fellow friends. She was a virgin, just like many others who were saving themselves for their spouse because it was the norm during that time. Mary appears to us as a reassuring image of God's Grace. She is an ordinary young woman under extraordinary favor.

Here are some insights that explain why Mary was an ordinary woman.

## CONCLUSION - LESSONS FROM MY STORY

1. Greetings are meant for people, no matter who they are.
2. Mary was confused and disturbed by what the angel told her.
3. Mary lived in a city like other young women.
4. Mary was troubled like any human being.
5. Mary was afraid like any other individual who saw something strange.
6. Mary showed her humanity by asking how she would conceive since she knew no man. She was not a deity; only God understands everything.
7. Mary hoped that everything the angel had told her would come to pass.
8. Mary trusted God.
9. Mary believed in God.
10. Mary was engaged to a carpenter.
11. Mary had relatives: a father, a mother, her cousin Elizabeth.

The Bible does not indicate the details of the life of Mary as a young woman. She might have been so excited, dreaming, making plans for the wedding ceremony like any other bride would do. This goes to show how Mary, an ordinary woman, was showered with the Grace of God, not because of who she was, but because of the goodness of God. Apart from Esther, there are also some other people whom the Scriptures say obtained God's favor. One of them was Esther.

> *"Now there was at the citadel of Susa a Jewish man from the tribe of Benjamin named Mordecai son of Jair, the son of Shimei, the son of Kish. He had been carried into exile from Jerusalem by Nebuchadnezzar king of Babylon among those taken captive with Jeconiah king of Judah.*
> 
> *And Mordecai had brought up Hadassah (that is, Esther), the daughter of his uncle because she did not have a father or mother. The young woman was lovely in form and appearance, and when her father and mother had died, Mordecai had taken her in as his daughter.*
> 
> *When the king's command and edict had been proclaimed, many young women gathered at the citadel of Susa under the care of Hegai.*

> *Esther was also taken to the palace and placed under the care of Hegai, the custodian of the women. And the young woman pleased him and obtained his favor, so he quickly provided her with beauty treatments and the special diet. He assigned to her seven select maidservants from the palace and transferred her with them to the best place in the harem."*
> **Esther 2:5-9**

Another ordinary woman who experienced the Grace of God was Esther. The story of Esther in the Bible is one of my favorite stories because it shows how God is not a respecter of persons. He does what He wants with whomever He wants. It does not depend on your social status, or your works, or anything you can imagine.

This is the story of a young Jewish girl named Hadassah, who was taken from her guardian, Mordecai, and forced to compete to become the king's wife. This unlikely contestant for a beauty pageant was crowned queen of Persia and renamed Esther, which means a "star."

Here are some points that make Esther an ordinary woman.

1. Esther was an orphan like many other orphans in the area at the time.
2. Esther was a virgin, just like all the other young women presented to the king of Persia.
3. Esther was beautiful, just like many other young women.
4. Esther was living a very modest life.
5. Esther was a refugee/immigrant.

> *Then Saul, still breathing threats and murder against the disciples of the Lord, went to the high priest and asked letters from him to the synagogues of Damascus, so that if he found any who were of the Way, whether men or women, he might bring them bound to Jerusalem.*
>
> *As he journeyed, he came near Damascus, and suddenly a light shone around him from heaven. Then he fell to the ground, and heard a voice saying to him, "Saul, Saul, why are you persecuting Me?"*
>
> *And he said, "Who are You, Lord?"*

## CONCLUSION - LESSONS FROM MY STORY

*Then the Lord said, "I am Jesus, whom you are persecuting. It is hard for you to kick against the goads."*

*So he, trembling and astonished, said, "Lord, what do You want me to do?"*

*Then the Lord said to him, "Arise and go into the city, and you will be told what you must do."*

*And the men who journeyed with him stood speechless, hearing a voice but seeing no one. Then Saul arose from the ground, and when his eyes were opened he saw no one. But they led him by the hand and brought him into Damascus. And he was three days without sight, and neither ate nor drank.*

*Ananias Baptized Saul Now there was a certain disciple at Damascus named Ananias; and to him the Lord said in a vision, "Ananias."*

*And he said, "Here I am, Lord."*

*So the Lord said to him, "Arise and go to the street called Straight, and inquire at the house of Judas for one called Saul of Tarsus, for behold, he is praying. And in a vision, he has seen a man named Ananias coming in and putting his hand on him so that he might receive his sight."*

*Then Ananias answered, "Lord, I have heard from many about this man, how much [b]harm he has done to Your saints in Jerusalem. And here he has authority from the chief priests to bind all who call on Your name."*

*But the Lord said to him, "Go, for he is a chosen vessel of Mine to bear My name before Gentiles, kings, and the children of Israel. For I will show him how many things he must suffer for My name's sake." Act 9:1-16*

"But by the grace of God I am what I am, and His grace toward me was not in vain; but I labored more abundantly than they all, yet not I, but the grace of God which was with me." (1 Corinthians 15:10)

"...of which I became a minister according to the gift of the grace of God given to me by the effective working of His power. To me, who am less than the least of all the saints, this grace was given, that I should preach among the Gentiles the unsearchable riches of Christ..." (Ephesians 3:7-8)

"Nevertheless, brethren, I have written more boldly to you on some points, as reminding you, because of the grace given to me by God, that I might be a minister of Jesus Christ to the Gentiles, ministering the gospel of God..." (Romans 15:15-16)

"But when it pleased God, who separated me from my mother's womb and called me through His grace, to reveal His Son in me, that I might preach Him among the Gentiles..." (Galatians 1:15)

"For our boasting is this: the testimony of our conscience that we conducted ourselves in the world in simplicity and godly sincerity, not with fleshly wisdom but by the grace of God, and more abundantly toward you." (2 Corinthians 1:12)

"And He said to me, "My grace is sufficient for you, for My strength is made perfect in weakness." Therefore, most gladly I will rather boast in my infirmities, that the power of Christ may rest upon me. Therefore, I take pleasure in infirmities, in reproaches, in needs, in persecutions, in distresses, for Christ's sake. For when I am weak, then I am strong." (2 Corinthians 12:9-10)

Who was Paul? He was a Roman citizen, which granted him respect wherever he went in the empire. He was a tentmaker by trade. He was persecuting the Jewish followers of Jesus. Saul was traveling to the city of Damascus when he saw a bright light and heard Jesus' voice saying, *"Saul, Saul, why do you persecute me?"* He fell from his horse, blinded. Days later, after a visit from Ananias, he recovered his eyesight and began to preach the gospel of Jesus Christ. Paul was an ordinary person, just like you and me.

Based on the above scriptures written by Paul, we understand that God is

## CONCLUSION - LESSONS FROM MY STORY

not a respecter of persons, and He is always willing to release and impart His Divine Grace upon the lives of those that trust and believe in Him.

For Paul to successfully carry out his divine purpose, he trusted that God would surround him with His Grace. Paul surrendered completely to the Lord and grasped a powerful secret and truth when he realized that his successes in ministry resulted from the pure Grace of God. Likewise, Mary and Esther experienced God's unmerited favor to simultaneously bear our Savior Jesus Christ and become the queen of Persia.

As it is evident from all the stories above that Mary, Esther, and Paul found favor in the eyes of God; we want to conclude that God is the source of Grace. The Bible reads in the Book of Psalm 84:11, *"For the Lord God is a sun and a shield; THE LORD WILL GIVE FAVOR and glory; No good thing will He withhold from those who walk uprightly."*

Therefore, the Grace of God does not manifest in your life because of your beauty, social position, and works but because of THE LORD. Let us go boldly to God, and we will undoubtedly find the favor that we need. The story of my pregnancies is my experience of God's Grace. It is evidence that Grace does not die; it is everlasting; it is still working and works on ordinary people. Grace can work on you too.

What are you going through right now? This book describes the working power of Grace and encourages believers to tap into the Grace of God that has been given freely. Moreover, it calls non-believers to submit their lives to the creator of the universe who can do above what they can ask or imagine, The One who is The Source of Grace.

## Comments I Heard After Sharing My Testimony

When I shared my story about giving birth without pain, some brothers and sisters in the faith reacted with disbelief to what the Lord had done.

1. "Come, come, come! You never felt any pain while giving birth?" She asked. "You need to get pregnant again and experience that pain. That

way, you will know what it feels like...."
2. "Even Mary, the one who bored Jesus, God himself in her womb had pain when she was giving birth to Jesus."
3. "Are you better than Mary, the mother of Jesus?"
4. "You might be the type of person that tolerates pain. Therefore, you cannot feel it."
5. "You are not normal! A normal woman will feel some pain while giving birth."
6. "What? No, no, no, it is not possible! Even the Bible says that the woman will give birth in pain."

Based on those comments, we understand that the Grace of God, when manifested in someone's life, causes reactions of awe or disbelief. It is important to realize that it is impossible to know the fullness of God. He is above everything and can do wonders. Our responsibility is to choose to yield and to receive. God's Grace does not depend on our achievements. Therefore, know ye now that it is available for you too; all you must do is RECEIVE.

# 11

# Testimonies

### Excerpt from Mama Mary Louise's Testimony

"Once we got to the hospital as the staff was waiting for us and had prepared a room, they had to dress her up in a hospital gown. They then plugged the devices in. To my surprise, I heard the nurse scream. But a big contraction just passed, and she was surprised that she did not feel it. Indeed, she always told me that she does not feel anything when she gives birth, that she always gave birth without pain, but I had not had the opportunity to be there when it happened. Then the nurse suggested that we should look at the device as she explained how to interpret the patterns. The labor went on. It was only through the device that we could tell she was in labor. The doctor himself was surprised. When the baby was about to come out, she started shaking so hard and sweating, and told me to sustain her neck. This is how you could tell something was going on inside of her body, but she felt absolutely nothing; there was the baby's head, and Grace was born. I will say that it's a phenomenon I cannot explain. The Lord knows how He creates His children and how He distributes his Grace to them."

## Excerpt from Jacinta's testimony

"She told me about her supernatural childbirth. When you haven't been pregnant it is a blessing to hear the other side because you always hear the bad things. Hers was very fast. Just the fact that she was texting and letting us know that she was having the baby when you know how other women scream... From what I heard from her I always received it every time she said to receive it when she shared her testimony. I can testify that she impacted my pregnancy. I wanted the one she had, I got something closer to that though I asked God for six hours. I gave birth so fast within two hours. I pray that the Lord uses Sandrine's testimony to bless other women. If it happened to her, it could happen to them too, because it happened to me. And for my next child, it will be like that, no pain."

And it came to pass. Jacinta gave birth to baby Joshua with no labor pains.

## Excerpt from Angeline's Testimony

"Sandrine introduced herself one night as my neighbor; I had just moved to that apartment. You know how when you move you are concerned about your neighborhood. Since she came to me first, she gained my trust. The following day, she invited me to their cell group (Bible study group), and I accepted to join the group. Not too long after she told me she was pregnant and started asking me questions about childbirth. She also told me that she was due. After asking me these questions, she later came back and told me she thought her water had broken. Since she had no pain, I thought there was no need for her to go to the hospital that soon. We waited for her husband and headed to the hospital.

When we got to the hospital, I kept touching her belly, so she could start labor. At some point, the nurse gave her a suppository, but nothing happened. However, the nurse told me that her labor was progressing, but it was weird because she had no pain. When I realized that she was not in pain, I decided to assess her. I started timing her labor as she said that she was hurting. She realized I was concerned and therefore decided to tell me what I wanted to hear. I started panicking and her husband as well. Later, because she realized that I and her husband were panicking, her blood pressure went high. When the doctor came to check her, he got concerned too, but the nurse assured him that she was fine, and suggested that I and her husband were the cause of the high blood pressure. The medical staff asked us to leave the room, to allow her to rest.

They were right because when we left, I assure you it was a miracle, I couldn't believe it. I could not understand. I thought she had a C-section. I was touched, with everything that I had seen, therefore I gave my life to Christ."

**Excerpt from Jacky's testimony**

"I have known Sandrine since 2007 through her husband, who was working in the same company as my husband. I learned a lot while being with her. This relationship changed my life. I remember that she used to testify about her births, how she gave birth like the Hebrew women. I was amazed and challenged at the same time because I wanted to live it. By the Grace of God, I have also experienced childbirth without pain, and this is because of her testimony. Today I can affirm that there are women on this earth that can give birth without pain. I have experienced it and I just want to give thanks to God."

**Excerpt from Chantal's testimony**

"I met Sandrine in the Bible school and became friends with her. I was taking care of her son while she was going to work.

She got pregnant with her second child. One night her water broke, and we went to the hospital. When we got to the hospital, the staff said that she could not give birth right away. But as soon as she laid down on the hospital bed, she gave birth without pain. It was a miracle because she was always claiming and confessing that she was going to give birth without pain, and even before the arrival of doctors, just like the Hebrew women. God performed that miracle in her life. After giving birth, she got sick, and we called Brother Marcel our Pastor to Pray for her. She got healed and we got out of the hospital. When you decide to follow God, He does miraculous things in your life. I give thanks to God."

# Salvation

If you have encountered the extravagant Grace of God after reading this book, but do not have a relationship with Him, I invite you today to make a decision to walk with Him and forever walk in that same grace as I have. God wants to use you in mighty ways, and it begins with a relationship with Jesus Christ.

To give your life to Jesus Christ means to repent of your sins, and accept the free gift of forgiveness through His sacrifice on the cross. The Bible says that no one gets to the Father except that they go through Jesus Christ (John 14:6), and I invite you today to pray this prayer and surrender your entire life to Him as your Lord and Savior.

> *Lord Jesus, I know I am a sinner, and today, I ask for your forgiveness for all my sins. I give you my life and surrender all that I am to follow You as my Lord and personal Savior. I ask that You fill me with your Holy Spirit so I can experience Your Extravagant Grace in all the days of my life. In Jesus' Name, Amen.*

As you have made your decision to follow Jesus Christ, I pray that you continue to choose to live for Him in order to fulfill the purpose for which He created you.

## About the Author

Sandy Bilong is a youth and young adults ministry leader at Harvest Intercontinental Ministry Olney in the Washington D.C. Area. She is passionate about uplifting and mentoring young people from all backgrounds. Having mentored and counseled thousands for more than 18 years, she believes that every young person on this earth has the potential of becoming the best version of themselves by God's Grace. She holds a Bachelor's degree in Education and a Master's in Healthcare Administration And Management.

She is a dedicated public servant of the Federal Government. She's also the mother of four wonderful children, Willy, Yvan, Joy, and Grace, and is the wife to Casimir Bilong. Her life's mission is to contaminate all those around her with the Grace of God.

**You can connect with me on:**
- https://extravagantgracebook.com
- https://www.facebook.com/sandrine.yembilong

www.ingramcontent.com/pod-product-compliance
Lightning Source LLC
Chambersburg PA
CBHW071840290426
44109CB00017B/1887